My Dear Dorothea . . .

My Dear Dorothea

A PRACTICAL SYSTEM OF

MORAL EDUCATION FOR FEMALES

EMBODIED IN A LETTER TO A

YOUNG PERSON OF THAT SEX

BY

Bernard Shaw

Illustrated by Clare Winsten

with a note by Stephen Winsten

Published by The Vanguard Press

New York

Introducing Dorothea,

Aunt Tabitha
seeks to improve you
by tracts.

My dear Dorothea,

As you have just completed your fifth year, a few words of wholesome counsel as to your conduct and feelings may not be unreasonable.

Pray do not be alarmed at a form of address so strange as "My dear Dorothea." I might have written "My dear little Dolly" as easily as your Aunt Tabitha. But I take no pleasure in spoiling a pretty name; and if you are little, it is not your fault. You wish to be a grown girl, and your ambition will not patiently bear to be reminded how far off is its consummation. Hard words, my dear Dorothea, which you would scarcely forgive me, did they not concern yourself.

You may perhaps wonder why I think it necessary to give you advice, whilst you are watched over by such excellent persons as Aunt Tabitha and godpapa Whenzentoul. I will tell you.

Aunt Tabitha seeks to improve you by tracts. You do not read the tracts, because you have discovered that they are somewhat dull. And you very properly dislike improvement, of which you do not feel the want.

Godpapa Whenzentoul hopes to gain your affection by taking you on his knee, asking you all sorts of questions, and hoping that you have been a good girl and will continue to be so. But as the questions are all silly ones, and you feel that they are made so purposely because you are little, you cannot help thinking that godpapa does not understand you.

Of course you intend to be a good girl always; and if in the past you may not have been quite faultless, you would rather not be spoken to about it. In short, Aunt Tabitha and godpapa are so good that they ought to be in heaven. They can never understand the affairs of a girl who would be terribly afraid to die tomorrow.

There are so many cross things in the world with which religion has nothing to do, that one sometimes wants almost bad advice. Or, at least, advice that can be taken.

It is just such advice, Dorothea, that I intend to offer you in this letter. I trust that it may profit you, and prepare you for the grim confusion into which you will descend, after you have successfully passed through the whooping cough, the scarlatina, the measles, and any other perilous experience which the infinite benevolence of the Omnipotent may impose upon you.

I need not now tell you in what respects you, a child of five years old, differ from your grown-up sisters, your nurse, your mother, or your governess. You know already that they are taller and stronger than you are; that they have money to spend; are allowed to walk about by themselves; habitually de-

Godpapa Whenzentoul
hopes to gain
your affection

There are few occupations which confer so much happiness as idolatry

ceive one another, and strangest of all, do not care either for dolls or sweetmeats. They have grown up completely in mind and body and are therefore expected to take care of themselves.

When you have reached your full height and finished all your lessons, you, too, will be left to your own guidance, thenceforth to do just as you like.

I need explain nothing of this to you at present, except to assure you that you will neither do, nor care to do, a single one of the many things which you have set your heart on doing in the day of your liberty. But I will tell you of some matters in which you are superior even to Aunt Tabitha.

There are few occupations which confer so much happiness as idolatry. You have learned from your tracts what idolatry is, and how wicked it is. However, as you do not usually regulate your doings by what the tracts say, we will say nothing more about them, except that they are printed by very silly people, and are by no means to be minded by little girls.

The poor Negro thinks that an image of stone can hear his prayers, and answer them. He makes believe so well, that he deceives himself; just as if you thought that your doll really said the pretty things you say for her.

Well, Dorothea, *you* are a little idolater! Would not the poor Negro shudder if I called his god a stone? Would you not hate me if I told you that

The poor Negro thinks
that an image of stone
can hear his prayers.

Aunt Tabitha was a foolish old maid, your mother a frivolous and selfish woman, your father a perverter of truth for gold, and the clergyman the worst man in church?

Yet, if you grow up a thoughtful girl, in a very few years some thoughts like these will begin to work in your mind, if, indeed, you do not before that suddenly hear Mrs. Whenzentoul calling godpapa names, and become a little unbeliever by the shock to your idolatry. For if they do such things, are not you, who believe them all to be so good and wise that they can neither commit a sin nor make a mistake, no better than an idolater? Such idolatry will bring you disappointment.

If your mother is always kind to you, love her more than you love anything except your doll; but never forget that she was once a little girl like yourself; that she is, as it were, yourself grown up; and that she is kind because she remembers how she liked people to be kind to her. If she is cross for a moment, recollect that you are sometimes cross yourself, and forgive her. As you know that she never wishes to cause you pain, you may without fear do whatever she tells you. If she tells you not to do something that you wish very much to do, you had better not do it; for she has seen so much more of people and things than you have, that you may be sure she knows some reason which you cannot understand, for which you should deny yourself what you wish.

You know more about
your doll
than anyone else.

Never on any account conceal anything from her or tell her what is not true. If you will think how much perplexed you would be if you could not be sure that whatever she said was the truth, you will understand what she would feel if she could not be certain that every word of yours was true, and see how foolish it would be to tell her a lie. Whenever you are uncertain what to do, ask her, but not until you have tried to think for yourself.

Always strive to find out what to do by thinking, without asking anybody. If you continually do this, you will soon act like a grown-up woman. For want of doing this, a very great number of grown-up people act like children.

If you cannot find out the right course for yourself, ask somebody. But be careful not to give yourself the habit of taking advice. You know so little at present that you must do many things because you are told to. But if you know anything about the matter, either decide for yourself or be sure that the person who advises you is right, before you follow the advice.

For instance, you know more about your doll than anyone else. If you are told to dress her in red, instead of going at once to do it, you must first consider whether she likes red; whether it suits her complexion; whether it is the fashion or not; and so on. Then, if you think it is the proper thing for her, dress her in it at once. But if not, let her alone; and remember for the future that the person who advised you to dress her in red knows nothing about dressing dolls.

By learning to decide for yourself, you will improve greatly, and will not have to be running continually to your mother when she is reading or sewing, and disturbing her with questions. You know how annoying it is to be disturbed when you are doing anything.

You must never annoy your mother. Always keep thinking how happy she is in having a pretty little daughter. She will think how pleasant it is for you to have a kind mother, and thus you will be a constant delight to one another.

If you had indeed such a mother, my dear Dorothea, you would not need my advice at all. But I must not forget how seldom little girls have such guardians; and I will therefore take it for granted that your mother, having long since exhausted the novelty of having a child of her own, thinks of you only as a troublesome and inquisitive little creature, whose dresses are continually torn and dirty, and whose face is too sticky to be kissed with pleasure.

For such a parent, you must be particularly careful not to form any warm affection. Be very friendly with her, because you are in the same house as she, and it is unpleasant to live with one whom you dislike. If you have any griefs, do not tell her of them. Keep them to yourself if possible, or if they are too bad for that, go to your nurse, if she is a kind one, or to the housemaid. But it is far bet-

There are robbers who
live in constant fear of Prison
yet they enjoy themselves very much indeed

ter to bear sorrow in silence. Other people have too many cares of their own to think much about yours.

If you observe this rule, you will not need to trouble your mother at all; and you will find that she will seldom trouble you, except by complaining when you make a noise, or telling you not to be naughty. These complaints you must bear patiently; but you may avoid many of them by keeping as much away from her as you can. You will soon be sent to school, and so get rid of her.

But there are some wicked women who beat their children; keep a constant watch over them. With such a mother it is very hard to be happy, but it is not impossible.

There are robbers who live in constant fear of prison, and who are forever hunted by soldiers and policemen; yet they enjoy themselves very much indeed. If your mother beats you, you must do as the robbers do.[1]

First of all you must learn not to hate her, and so you will be delighted at occurrences which other girls cry over. When she forbids you to do anything, try as hard as you can to do it without being found

[1] On the subject of child beating, see Proverbs XIII: 24; XIX: 18; XXII: 15; XXIII: 13, 14; and XXIX: 15, strongly advocating the practice. It may fairly be assumed that Solomon practiced his own principles. The result may be seen in the career of his son Rehoboam, narrated in II Chronicles X, XI, and XII; I Kings XII, XIV. G. B. Shaw.

If she leaves any
marks on you,
show them to
all visitors

out. But be careful to be very good with people who treat you well, to show that your wickedness is not natural to you.

If she leaves any marks on you, show them to all the people who come to the house and complain to everybody of the way in which she uses you. This will make them dislike her, and be sorry for you. When you are in church, pretend to fear that she is going to beat you, and ask her not to do so in a loud voice. If she tries to make you do anything by threatening, refuse to do it; because if she finds she can make you obedient by beating you, she will be constantly doing so.

No matter what pain it costs you, try and be brave. If you succeed, people will be afraid to offend you. And no matter how angry you may feel, strive always to be gentle and kind to those who treat you well; and everybody will wish to have you for a friend. Always remember that you must not act injuriously yourself. If anybody hurts you, and you think that they are not really fond of hurting you, but only a little passionate, you may forgive them after a while if you like.

In the pages which you have read, I have given you some hints as to your behavior at home. I have done so by inventing different sorts of mothers for you: a good one, an ordinary one, and a bad one. But as there are many more than these three kinds, I will have to leave you to yourself now as to your treatment of your family. You will soon be going to school, where you will have no relatives, but where you will find friends whom you will like far more. I trust you will find the advice I am now about to give you, useful everywhere. And in order to get over the most tiresome topics at once, I will begin by advising you on the subject of Religion.

When people ask you whether you read your Bible, say that you do, and though you will be telling them stories, they will deserve it for asking questions that do not concern them. You need not think about religion until you are grown up; because you would not understand it. You need not be in the least afraid of going to hell, and if you avoid thinking about it, and be careful not to read "good" books, you will spare yourself much discomfort, and keep yourself in good health.

There is, however, one good book which you ought to read, because it is a very pleasant story: *Pilgrim's Progress*. You must read this before you are ten years old. Be sure and do not let your opportunity slip. If you are told that any book is not fit for you to read, get it and read it when nobody is looking. There are some books that are not fit for grown-up people; but all books are fit for you. Therefore read everything except what you find tiresome. Fairy tales are the prettiest of all, but you will find that the men who make the pictures seldom make the princesses pretty enough or the goblins ugly enough. Story books are much better than lesson

you are told that any book is not fit for you to read, get it, read it.

When all fools talk
at the same time
The wise people
cannot be heard

books. They teach you more, and are much pleasanter to read.

Let your rule of conduct always be to do whatever is best for yourself. Be as selfish as you can. And here I feel that I must stop to explain something to you. In reading this letter, you have been surprised at finding directions quite opposite to those which you are accustomed to receive. I will perhaps surprise you still more when I tell you that what everybody says is almost sure to be wrong. The reason is, that there are far more fools in the world than wise people; and when all the fools talk, as they often do, the wise people cannot be heard.

And even the wise people give wrong advice because they forget their own childhood, and think that children have no sense. But you, my dear Dorothea, know better than that. You often understand what the grown-up people are talking about, when they fancy that you are too young to mind them. I know how clever you are, and I advise you just as I would an older person. And so far, I feel sure you have found my advice to be, on many points, very natural and proper. Otherwise I could not ask you to follow it without contradicting the warning I gave you a few pages back about the proper manner of treating advice.

I will now return to what I have to say to you concerning Selfishness. When you make up your mind to be very selfish, you must be quite sure that you know how to be so. Some girls think, for instance, that greedy people are selfish. This is not the case. They are only silly people trying to be selfish without knowing how. They make themselves ill, and are disliked by those who live with them; and the bad opinion of those around them makes them so unhappy, that they never enjoy themselves except when they are eating. And it is surely very silly to prevent oneself from having more than two pleasant hours in the long day.

You will often feel tempted to take things that you want very badly, from people who are weaker than you. But you must not do so, because there are others who are stronger than you; and if everyone were to seize what he desired by force, you would be very miserable. This consideration for the consequences of one's acts is called Duty. You have often been told to do your Duty; but most likely you do not quite know what it means. Therefore I will try and explain it to you.

You must know that this world in which we live is a very badly arranged one. Some people are born with a great deal more money and clothes than others; some are even born without any at all. Everybody likes money and clothes, and the consequence is, that the people who have none want to take some from the people who have plenty; and the people who have plenty are angry because they have not as much as the Queen. But if they were to steal

whatever they wanted, and hurt those with whom they were angry, the world would be so full of thieves and murderers that nobody could live happily in it.

As everybody wishes to be happy, they make an agreement together that each man and woman will keep whatever he or she has. They also agree that they will not strike or kill one another, and if any person breaks the agreement and robs, strikes, or murders another, all the rest shut him up in prison to prevent him from doing so any more. They do this by paying some men to watch for evil-doers and catch them: and the men who are paid are called policemen. I am sure you have seen them in the park talking to your nurse.

You have a part in this agreement just as everybody else has, and this part is called your Duty. "Do unto others as you would have them do to you" is a common rule for doing your duty. However, you need, for the present, only take care not to do unto others anything that you would not wish others to do to you. Duty is a very tiresome thing to read about; but it is necessary to say something to you on the subject, in order to show you that you are to be good-natured and gentle, not because you are told to be so (which is a very ridiculous reason indeed) but because it is the best way to avoid the unhappiness of which the world is so full. If you act otherwise, you will be told quite truly that you are forgetting yourself; and this you must never do.

Do unto others as you would have them do unto you is a common rule for doing your duty

Always have the highest respect for yourself, and you will be too proud to act badly.

You are, if you will excuse my saying so, an extremely discontented Dorothea. And yet, how often have you been told by Aunt Tabitha that it is sinful to be discontented? How many times has godpapa Whenzentoul assured you that a contented mind is a continual feast? "But," you may ask me, "how do you know that I am discontented?" Very easily indeed, my dear Dorothea. Because no one is contented.

It may surprise you, but there is no such thing as contentment in the world. You must not place too much faith in grown-up people. They are always pretending to be better than they are. Aunt Tabitha is not really and truly contented. She is unhappy because she is not married. If she were married, she would wish herself single again. Your godpapa is always wishing for more money. I confess to you that I am discontented.

Some of the holiest men have been terribly unhappy.[1] King Solomon, who first spoke of a merry heart as having a continual feast, wrote a book so full of grief that you would almost cry if you read it. Elijah the prophet, a good man who never died, but went straight up to heaven in a horse-and-car, asked God to kill him because he could not bear to live. Jesus Christ was so melancholy that he never

[1] See Proverbs xv: 15; Ecclesiastes; 1 Kings xix: 4.
G. B. Shaw.

I confess to you
that I am discontented

smiled, or took any amusement, except some boating occasionally.

You have been told so often that contentment is a good thing, that you will probably feel sorry and disappointed to hear that it has no existence. But if you think about it for a minute, you will perceive that in reality it would destroy all your pleasure if you possessed it. The reason why people praise it so much is, that it is natural to them to esteem the things they have not and to despise the things they have, just as you often think that other dolls are prettier than your own. But, in truth, your doll is the prettiest one I ever saw; and in the same way, Discontent would be praised above all things, if people only gave it the credit it deserves.

If you were quite contented, think how many pleasures you would lose, and how slovenly you would look! You would never wash your face or hands, because you would be content to remain dirty. A new dress would give you no pleasure, because you would be content with the old one. You would not learn to read or write; and you would be so contented with bread that you would take no pleasure in eating a Bath bun.

You would be an uncleanly, ignorant, and unlovable child if you were contented. Therefore be glad that you are discontented, and try to remain so. Never think yourself clever enough or neat enough, and you will always be learning more and improving in your appearance. And when older people preach content-

King Solomon
wrote a book
so full of grief that you
would almost cry
if you read it.

Elijah the prophet,
a good man,
went straight up
to heaven
in a horse-and-
car.

ment to you, you may be sure they are either thought-less or hypocritical.

You must not be surprised when you meet with hypocrites. The world is so full of them that in the course of your life you will scarcely discover one person who does not sometimes say things he does not mean, or pretend to be greatly concerned about affairs that do not at all affect him. What is still more surprising is, that if you do meet such a person, you will not like him. I say "him," because he would certainly be a man. There are some men who always say what they think, no matter how unpleasant it may be; but there never was a woman yet who did so.

Hypocrisy is just like Selfishness. It is only bad when it is improperly used. I tried to explain to you before that it can never be your real interest to be greedy, cruel, or rude; and that though wicked people are called selfish, they do not really enjoy themselves as those who are selfish in the proper way. It is just so with Hypocrisy.

It is a very excellent thing to be properly hypo-critical. And it is very easy to find out what hypocrisy is proper: it is that which may please, but cannot injure. I will give you an example: suppose you had a kind friend who died. You would be very sorry for your loss, and you would feel (knowing how kind the friend was) that everyone else ought to be sorry too. And if your companions laughed at your grief, you would feel hurt. By this you may

You must not be surprised when you meet with hypocrites

perceive that when those whom you meet tell you that they have lost their friends, you must, in order to avoid paining them, look as sorrowful as possible.

This will be an act of hypocrisy on your part, but a very proper and kind one. You must also pretend to think that all your acquaintances' dead friends are in heaven, although you may privately feel quite certain that they are in hell. Indeed, you may lay it down as a rule for practicing Hypocrisy, that unpleasant things which you may know about people should never be mentioned.

You will meet many ladies and gentlemen who tell lies, steal hairpins and umbrellas, curse and swear, get drunk, beat each other, and pretend that their parents were much grander people than they really were; but in speaking of them and to them, you must seem to think that they are quite honest, gentle, and modest.

They have a right to do as they please; and if they are foolish enough to behave badly, that is no business of yours, so long as they do not injure you. But you may observe how such people are disliked and spoken ill of, in order to convince yourself of how little they know how to be selfish.

Never make remarks about the dresses of your mamma's visitors, nor play with anything that belongs to them. And do not talk much or scream whilst they are in the room. If you are careful about these things, they will most likely ask you to their houses, and give you cake. However, do not ask them for cake, or for anything else whatever. If people want to give you anything, they will not need to be asked. When they do give you something, you must be hypocritical again and pretend to like it much more than you really do. It will do you no harm, and perhaps encourage them to give you other things.

Nothing is more important to your happiness than the habit, which you must try to form, of never wishing for anything that you cannot either buy or make for yourself. Everybody in this world is expected to take care of himself, and live without asking help from his fellow creatures. Even those things which are done for you by your parents because you are so little, such as buying your food and clothes, are only done on condition that when you have little children of your own, you will do the same for them.

Therefore, never ask anything as a favor, but only those things which you are entitled to have, or which you have deserved by your conduct. If this should sometimes prove hard to abide by, remember that the world is an unhappy place, and that it is only made bearable by each person agreeing to bear some share of trouble. No matter how heavy a load is, its weight is scarcely felt when it is divided among many persons.

Every person must bravely take his share, and

you must take yours. When you see others wanting to escape their little portion of the great burden, by begging from others, or refusing to repay their politeness, you may despise them, and feel that you have a greater claim to respect than they.

This leads me to the subject of Pride. Pride, which makes us desire to appear to the best advantage on every point, is a feeling which should be kept in check rather than encouraged. As long as you take pride only in those qualities or properties which you possess, you will be the happier for it. But unfortunately, you are but too prone to think little of that which you have, and to covet what is beyond your reach.

Once you covet a thing, you will hate to be reminded that you have not got it. If you can do so without being found out, you will pretend to have it. This desire for things or affectation of qualities which you can never possess, arises from a sort of pride which cannot fail to make you unhappy. In order to use a word already familiar to you, I will call it Vanity.

People are most commonly vain about beauty and family. Whatever your birth may be, or whatever your face is like, remember that you cannot alter it: so it is useless to spend a moment in grieving over either the one or the other. Although, as I have said, it is apt to lead to certain vices, such as Vanity, Pride is a very useful sentiment. It is the main source of

Discontent, and I have already shown you how excellent a thing that is.

Your pride will make you wish to know as much as other people, to look as well, and to behave as nicely. And here you must carefully think of how much of this is Pride, and how much is Vanity. Suppose you have a playmate who speaks French, who has pretty eyes, and whose manner with strangers is nice; and that you wish to be equal to her in these matters. You must make up your mind to learn French, because she has learned it, and as she has learned it, so can you. That is proper pride.

But never mind her eyes or her manner. She was born with them, and has them quite by accident. You may have heard of learning manners, and I mention it to you the more particularly because there is nothing which girls envy one another more than their manners. But a person's manner is a part of herself. Perhaps you have noticed that though everybody has a face with a nose on it, and the same number of eyes, arms, legs, and fingers; yet no two people are exactly alike. Just in the same way, a hundred little girls at a party will observe the same rules of behavior. They will all curtsey to the lady of the house, and eat as much cake as their parents will allow them to; they will not eat with their knives, drink tea out of their saucers, or take bones in their hands to gnaw the flesh from; and still each will have quite a different manner.

The men
who make pictures
seldom make
the princesses pretty enough
or the goblins ugly enough

Everybody has a
with a nose on it and
the same number of e
arms, legs and fingers
yet no two peop
are exactly alike

Some will be disagreeable, some will be sleepy; a few will sit primly and look very old. There will be some shy girls who do not enjoy themselves, and many merry and talkative ones who do. Remember then, that though your behavior may be as proper as that of any other girl, your manner can never be the same, any more than your nose can. This strange difference to everyone else need not make you feel uncomfortable or lonely; for it is your most valuable possession. It is called your Individuality.

The name is so long that you will find it easy to remember. Many persons are so ignorant of the value of their individuality, that they spend their lives in weakening it by imitating others. At last they lose it: and as it is impossible for them to get a new one, they have nothing but the color of their clothes and their outside shape to distinguish them from one another.

You will meet an immense number of such people in the world. They are described by various names, such as commonplace, ordinary, highly respectable, and the like. I am sure you would not like to be called commonplace. Therefore you must preserve your Individuality by never imitating others, or pretending to be what you are not.

Also remember constantly this rule: the more you think for yourself, the more marked will your Individuality be. The more you allow others to think for you, the more you will resemble others. And just think how shocking the world would be if all people were as much alike as soldiers in a box are.

By always considering what is proper Pride, and what mere Vanity, you will learn to distinguish those qualities or accomplishments with which persons are born and which are therefore a part of their Individuality from those which are acquired by study or practice. Those who have good natural gifts are fortunate, but they deserve no credit for them. This you will easily remember; but you are likely to forget that those who have no natural gifts, but are born poor or ugly, or both, are not therefore to be blamed or despised.

Ridiculous though it may seem to you, my dear Dorothea, the scullery maid is every whit as good a person as you are, unless you can surpass her by learning more, by being kinder and controlling your temper better, and by doing work that requires more thought than washing dishes. Such superiority alone deserves admiration and respect. No matter how rich, how clever, or how beautiful you may be, all these will only make you wretched unless you teach yourself many other things besides.

To learn is often troublesome, but any trouble is worth taking that will make you happier when you grow up. I will tell you some of the qualities which you must especially strive to teach yourself.[1]

The first and most important is called Self-control. Never cry, and never lose your temper. Of all the

[1] Proverbs XVI: 29; XVI: 32.   G. B. Shaw.

The scullery maid
is every whit
as good a person
as you are

counsel which I have written down here for you, these two precepts are the chief; because if you neglect them, you cannot follow the rest. Crying is the worst habit you can possibly form. It spoils your appearance, and only gratifies those who inflict pain on you. If you cry for trifles, you will not be able to avoid crying on more serious occasions. Tears are only useful in exciting the compassion of persons who have something which you wish them to give you. And surely you would not care to receive a gift, as a bone is flung to a troublesome dog, merely to get rid of an annoyance.

Some girls cry because they desire to be petted. Such girls are silly, peevish, and unable to live without being helped. You must learn to live without any assistance; to help others rather than seek help for yourself; and to bear sorrow without floods of tears or any pitiful display of grief.

Never give anyone a reason for despising you. Those who see you weeping will either despise you or pity you. And pity is akin to contempt.

When you have learned to control your tears, you will have made a great advance in the art of keeping your temper. And from this art you will derive so many advantages, that I do not think you would have the patience to listen to half of them, if I attempted to describe them to you. But I must explain to you what keeping your temper really is, lest you should mistake its meaning, and be discouraged.

People only lose their temper when they are angry. Therefore they think that in order to keep their temper, they must not get angry. But this is absurd; for people cannot help being angry when they are offended. It is when your anger makes you forget what you are doing, that your temper is lost. Then you say or do things which you are sorry for or ashamed of afterwards; you look like a savage or a wild cat; and everybody, seeing you in such a state, believes you to be in the wrong.

You gain nothing at all to make up for this; so you may see clearly that you will not only do well to keep your temper, but that by doing so you will have a great advantage in any dispute over others who may not equal you in self-control.

This self-control is very much the same thing as Patience, but you need only be patient in enduring evils that cannot be remedied. If another girl slaps your face, you must not be patient, as she would probably only be encouraged to repeat the assault. But you must make it a rule never to slap anyone who does not attack you. Do not, even when you are struck, lose your temper; because you would say rude things.

You must always be polite, particularly to those whom you dislike; because politeness is a mark of superiority; and in order to make unpleasant people respect you, you should endeavor to appear as superior to them as possible.

Servants, in particular, must be politely spoken to.

If you are rudely spoken to, show your better sense by replying politely. But avoid the acquaintance of rude persons. They have no right to be spoken to by anyone, since they do not choose to make themselves agreeable.

Never contradict or fight with people when you can possibly help it. It is annoying, and spoils the pleasure of the whole day.

If you are beaten by a person bigger and stronger than you are, ask somebody to protect you. When a strong person oppresses a weak one, it is said to be Tyranny. As long as you live, resist tyranny; and never be guilty of it yourself. Never hurt those weaker than yourself, and try to prevent others from doing it. But do not be too fond of mixing in other people's quarrels. And before you resent ill-treatment as tyranny, make sure that you have not brought it upon yourself.

The time is fast approaching when your scholastic education will commence. You will either be taught by a governess, or sent to school. If the former, you will attend to the principles which I have already laid down, and shape your course according to circumstances. I could not tell you how to treat a private teacher. All governesses are different.

Schools, on the contrary, are all more or less alike. Therefore it may not be amiss to give you a few hints as to your behavior when you enter one. At home, you are accustomed to a certain amount of attention and protection, which prevents your having to take care of yourself to any great extent. On leaving it for school, you will find yourself suddenly in the midst of a barbarous community. They will not care at all about you.

The school discipline, to which you are unused, will be irksome. Knowing nobody, and feeling uncertain whom to trust, you will feel lonely, and wish heartily that you might go home again. Console yourself by remembering that this will only last a week, and let nothing tempt you to let any girl know what you feel.

Pretend to be cheerful; and when you come to know your schoolfellows, to pick out those whom you like, and to feel as if you belonged to the place, you will laugh at your former grief. But do not forget it so far when you are no longer a new girl as to laugh at other girls whom you see looking sorrowful, or even crying, during their first few days' experience of school life.

In your behavior towards the school, you must be guided by what I have already told you. Do not quarrel or speak rudely, as all the rest so often do; injure nobody; and revenge at once and as severely as you can any injury which you may receive without having provoked.

Remember that the schoolmistress is the natural enemy of all, and never on any account tell tales to her. No matter how badly any girl treats you, never complain of her unless she is much bigger than you

and you cannot find any other remedy. It is better to do without sweets than to ask the housemaid to get them for you, because to do so would be to place yourself in her power.

If any girl threatens to tell the schoolmistress of anything you do, tell her she may do so if she likes. If she does, try and fasten the name of telltale on her; and even warn the others against her. If the mistress punishes you, you must submit with an appearance of indifference. The less you seem to care, the more you will annoy her.

But on no account permit her to strike you. Attend to your lessons as much as you can without fatiguing yourself; and get into mischief as often as you can. This will give you the habit of working and enjoying yourself at the same time.

Never listen to religious instruction. I have already promised to write to you on that subject when you are old enough to care about it.

This letter is now so long, that you will hardly have patience to finish it at a single reading. Nor is it my intention that you should do so. Keep it and read it occasionally. The older you grow, and the better you know the world, the more easily you will understand it. If its precepts are of use to you when you are five years old, they will be equally so when you are thirty-five.

Give my respectful compliments to your Aunt

Tabitha, and remember me to your excellent god-papa, Mr. Whenzentoul. They may not find that my reflections on education have been conceived in a spirit familiar to them. They will at least admit that the system of which they approve is neither so consistent in its application, nor so uniformly successful in its results, as to warrant a universal adoption of it.[1]

At some future stages of your career, I may again address you on the great subject of yourself. Till then, be assured that I will continue to feel for you the romantic affection of a parent, tempered by the rational interest of an experimental philosopher.

G. B. Shaw

---

[1] "There is a way that seemeth right unto a man, but the end thereof are the ways of death." Proverbs XVI: 32; XIV: 12. This cuts both ways.   G. B. Shaw.

Editorial Note

This piece was the first serious literary effort of Bernard Shaw. It was written in 1878, in his twenty-first year and soon after he arrived in London. He had burned his boats by throwing up a good post as cashier in a Land Agency and was now trying his luck as artist or author.

He left Dublin because it was an art Sahara, but his regular routine had instilled the habit of work. Now, instead of collecting rents, he went from meeting to meeting collecting ideas; instead of keeping accounts he worked out the prospects of an artist or author in the contemporary world: it was a form of literary accountancy. After months of reckoning he came to the conclusion that all the arts were exhausted, that the giants had used up all the aesthetic resources and had left no room for newcomers. His response was: the arts are dead, long live the arts.

There was one art which had been neglected, the art of living. His own upbringing had been completely anarchic. As an example of parental competence to guide, educate, and develop children, his parents had been laughably absurd; his sister's reaction to this was to adore everything commonplace and conventional; Bernard's was just the opposite. He thought things out for himself from first principles and refused to ignore unpalatable facts. It was obvious that he was deeply influenced in his approach to humanity by Bunyan's *Pilgrim's Progress*.

In this Open Letter we watch him thinking aloud and feeling his way to an intimacy with the reader. In order to express his thoughts in the simplest language, he pretends to be addressing himself to a girl of five for whom he feels "the romantic affection of a parent, tempered by the rational interest of an experimental philosopher." Most of the conclusions arrived at stayed with him for the remainder of a long and active life, and if we were not aware of the fact that it was written in 1878, we might have been deceived into thinking that he was quoting his own plays and prefaces. In fact, this piece is the very quintessence of all his work and may well be regarded as the germinating ground of his genius. It certainly transfigured a person "doomed by heredity to futility" into the person he became.

It will read to many as a most timely piece. It might well have provoked the recent Curtis Committee report on the care of children deprived of parental affection and which resulted in the Children's Act of 1948. Even in *The Times* of today's date, seventy-eight years after Shaw had written his letter to "My dear Dorothea," our attention is called to the fact that there are still children who are cruelly treated.

My Dear Dorothea marks the turning point in the attitude to children: the realization that they have thoughts and dreams of their own. Here the young Dubliner shows an uncanny understanding of the child mind; and though his remedies are often to be deplored, his relationship with the child is wholly healthy and happy. What child would not consider the possession of a parent like the writer of the long letter a possession greater even than a doll? And many a reader may well think that of all the hundreds of characters created by George Bernard Shaw, this one is the most revealing.

S. W.